I love Andalusia
travel guide

By S. L. Giger as *SwissMiss on Tour*

"Blessed are the curious for they shall have adventures."
– Lovelle Drachman

Receive a free packing list

Never forget anything important ever again and don't waste unnecessary time with packing. Scan the QR code and receive a free packing list along with a sample of my Thailand travel guide.

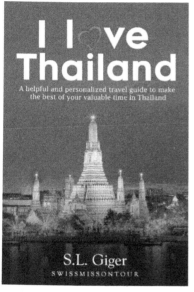

Content

Why should I choose this guidebook instead of any other?

Do you only have a limited amount of time (like two or three weeks) and feel a bit overwhelmed about which places you should visit? Should you spend more time in the culture-rich city of Sevilla, exploring the beaches of the Costa del Sol, or visiting Moorish castles? Andalusia offers a big variety of stunning places that it might be difficult to choose and settle on a route. This guidebook will help you to focus on the must-sees of Andalusia. Marvel at incredible views across rolling green hills with ancient monuments, taste delicious tapas and wines, study paintings by world-famous artists, surf in the Atlantic Ocean or the Mediterranean Sea, and visit the best cities Andalusia has to offer. *I love Andalusia* will tell you about the best spots. It also mentions the must-dos in Madrid since it's the awesome capital of Spain and you might be flying to Madrid and then travel to Andalusia anyway.

With *I love Andalusia*, you won't have to do any further research. You find a two-week travel itinerary with detailed "how-to"-guidelines and further ideas and descriptions.

Do you want to plan your own, smooth journey in Andalusia? This guidebook will help you to do just that. You will get to know the advantages or disadvantages of renting a car or traveling by public transport with distance and time indications for all the routes between places.

In case you are worried about the Spanish language, there is a small language guide with helpful words at the end of this book. Indeed, it is an advantage if you speak at least a touristy amount of Spanish. Therefore, I will also tell you about the app with which I successfully learned Spanish. However, in case you don't feel like learning a new language, you should be fine with some English, hands, feet, and Google Translate.

Woohoo, time to start planning, enjoy your holiday in Andalusia!

Reasons to look forward to your journey in Andalusia in case you are not entirely convinced yet

Probably, this chapter is a bit superfluous since Andalusia has long made a name for itself. It attracts tourists with its rich cultural heritage and delicious tapas or wine. Yet, not only because of the food you are in for a treat when traveling in Andalusia. Spain may be one of the most loved tourist destinations of Europeans, nevertheless you still find stretches of beautiful empty beaches in Andalusia. Moreover, you have such a huge selection of great cities like Malaga, Seville, Cordoba, and Cadiz that the tourist masses spread out and you still get to witness enough of the local culture. That's why I always love returning to Spain and visiting more interesting places or revisiting my favorite cities. So, it's pretty likely that you will also fall in love with Spain, and after going to Andalusia, you might already be dreaming about when to go back and explore more of Spain.

Andalusia Highlights

I'm always asked what my favorite place in a country was. It's a difficult question because there are usually just too many beautiful places. In Andalusia, a lot of beautiful sights will amaze you and it was not an easy task to choose the best three. However, here are my three highlights of the province of Andalusia.

1. Puente Nuevo in Ronda

This bridge is such a special landmark that you must see it with your own eyes.

2. The Alhambra and the Generalife in Granada

There are many buildings in Andalusia that have an Arabic heritage. However, if you have time to only visit one of those monuments, it has to be this one. It's the biggest of the Moorish palaces that you can visit, and it greatly shows the nice architectural features and the beautiful gardens.

3. Plaza de España in Sevilla

Sevilla is a must-visit on your trip through Andalusia since it's a beautiful city that offers you all the traditions of Spain like Flamenco and tapas. In addition, the most beautiful square of Spain (at least in my opinion) is located in Sevilla. On Plaza de España you find Venecian like bridges with a canal and even row boats as well as beautiful ceramic tile benches. Their pictures represent all the regions of Spain and hence you can take a short trip through the whole country and its islands by visiting Plaza de España.

Things to consider before you visit Andalusia to have the best possible trip

Here are the things you need to know in order to have a smooth journey.

Currency

Spain uses the Euro. The short form is EUR or €. At the time of writing this book, 1 EUR equaled 1.10 USD. You can determine the current exchange rate, for example by typing USD to EUR in the Google search bar.

Almost anywhere you can also pay by debit card or with a credit card, except perhaps at a vegetable stand. For that, it's good to bring a little cash.

Drinking water

Tap water in Spain tastes terrible and opinions on the Internet were divided about whether it had a good enough quality to drink or whether it contained substances that would boost cancer cells or other sicknesses. Better only drink it if there is a water filter installed at the tap or bring your own travel water filter.

The hotel staff told me that the water is drinkable in most major cities if you are not fussy about taste. On the Canary Islands, tap water really isn't drinkable and will give you stomach problems if you drink it anyway.

Best time to travel

The best time to travel in Andalusia is spring and fall, so April/May/June and September/October. Temperatures are agreeable but not sizzling hot.

In July and August, it's the best time to just hang out at the beach. However, walking around the cities and visiting one sight after the other might give you a heat stroke if you don't take a siesta at the hottest hours of the day.

Since it's still sunny in winter, the cities and beaches of Andalusia are also attractive in winter. However, it can be that even if the weather report says that there will be a maximum temperature of 18 degrees Celsius, it will feel like 8 degrees. The sun just isn't that strong. So, bring a packable down jacket if you travel to Andalusia between November and February.

Visa and Vaccinations

No visa is required to enter Spain and you can visit Spain without a visa for up to 90 days. This will change at the beginning of 2024 when the Schengen area starts the ETIAS Visa Waiver program. It will be similar to the US ESTA Visa, and you can apply for it online for a period of 3 years: www.spainvisa.eu/visa-types/tourist-visa/etias-visa/

The following nationalities already need a visa now, when coming to Spain and can apply for it on the website of the Spanish embassy: Afghanistan, Bangladesh, D.R. Congo, Eritrea, Ethiopia, Ghana, Iran, Iraq, Nigeria, Pakistan, Somalia, and Sri Lanka.

Vaccinations

Spain does not require you to get any mandatory vaccinations. However, routine vaccinations like Measles-Mumps-Rubella (MMR), Chickenpox (Varicella), and Diphtheria-Tetanus-Pertussis are recommended. About the covid vaccine, you can read in the chapter about covid measures.

How to stay safe in Spain

Spain generally is a safe country that is used to tourists. Therefore, your only dangers are pickpockets and bicycle thieves, in case you rent a bicycle and don't lock it well.

Here are some safety tips, so that you will still have all your belongings at the end of your trip to Andalusia.

- **Be alert of your surroundings when you are in crowded areas**

Pickpockets will do their work on buses or markets when you are busy sampling fruit or trying to figure out which stop you have to get off. Then, better wear your backpack in front of you if you have anything valuable inside it. In addition, during the times you are not using your phone, don't just stick it into your back pocket or open jacket pocket as that seems like an invitation to take it from you. Hide it in your bag or at least close the zipper of your jacket pocket.

- **Don't wear expensive jewelry**

Of course, you can wear whatever you want but if you make yourself appear like you have nothing worth robbing, you are also less likely a target.

- **Spread your money**

Don't keep all your cards and money in one wallet. Spread them across several places of your luggage. Only always bring as much money as you think you will need for the time you will spend out of the accommodation.

- **Walk around with a plastic bag or cheap shopping bag**

Instead of an expensive-looking purse or camera bag, just bring your camera or anything else you carry with you in a cheap shopping bag. I traveled through South America with a free, reusable shopping bag and sometimes carried my laptop around in it while nobody would have expected that.

With those tips, I hope you will only experience the positive sides of Spain.

Covid regulations

Because everything changes so quickly regarding Covid, I can't give you general travel advice for it. I strongly hope that by the time you are reading this book, Covid won't rule over the travel industry anymore. However, if Covid regulations are still in place, there are three things you need to check:

1. What regulations does Spain currently have? Can your nationality enter the country? Do you need proof of a test or a vaccine?
The current requirements for Spain can be checked on this website: https://spainguides.com/latest-spain-entry-require-ments/
You might need proof of vaccination or recovery or a negative test result. In addition, you might need to fill in an online health form which will generate a QR code for you that you have to present at the airport.

2. Are there any obligations when returning to your country?
You might need to get an antigen test or a PCR test and perhaps Spain is on your countries quarantine list. In Spain, it was easy to get tested at the airport or in pharmacies. They checked my certificate before entering the plane.

3. Do you need a test or vaccine for the airline you are flying with or because of the stopover you are having?
Best contact the airline for information about that if you aren't sure.

Finding your way

As everywhere I go, I used the **maps.me** app on my phone and downloaded Spain for offline use. This has been a very useful companion every day and always brought me to the place I wanted to go. You can use it to find points of interest within a city, to get to your accommodation, or to follow a hiking route (for example at Caminito del Rey). Tourists can mark spots and write comments. Hence you can even discover secret spots which other tourists recommend.

Wi-Fi

Public Wi-Fi in Spain was often shaky or not usable at all. This was above all an inconvenience at Madrid airport and in some restaurants. However, for me, that's not reason enough to extra purchase roaming data or a second sim card. I got by fine because all of our accommodations offered free and reliable Wi-Fi.

How to pick your accommodation

Since travelers all have their individual preferences about what standard their accommodation needs to be, I think it's best if you check the various options on **booking.com**. There, you also have all the latest reviews for the hostels and can get an opinion about a place before getting there. The best deals

you usually get by directly booking on the website of the accommodation or by reaching genius level on booking.com.
However, I mentioned some hotels in this guide since I had a really incredible experience there.
If you want more local experiences, you should look for gems on **Airbnb**.

Usually, I only book one night and if I like the place, I extend my stay. Of course, this doesn't work during local holidays and other special occasions.

Book your accommodation through me

Since recently, I have access to the booking platforms, with which travel agencies work. That's why I could find better hotel deals for you. If you are interested, send me an e-mail (swissmissontour@gmail.com) with the dates

and your desired hotel (with or without breakfast?) or the desired city and your budget and I can check the price for you or book your nights directly. However, I have noticed that it is more worthwhile for 4- or 5-star hotels. The cheaper hotels have such a small margin that the prices on the hotel website or Booking.com are sometimes the same or cheaper than the prices on the business booking platforms.

Introductory offer: If you book three or more nights through me, I will send you another travel guide (of mine) of your choice free of charge as an e-book. This applies to hotel bookings around the world.

Learn Spanish

For Spain, it's not necessary to speak Spanish in order to get by, since they are used to tourists and often speak English, French or the hotel staff even German. Yet, it has a big effect on the locals if you utter the first words you say to them in Spanish. They will appreciate your effort and quickly, you become friends.

I first started learning Spanish with the free Duolingo app. However, I just didn't make any progress with it as there was so much unnecessary vocabulary that you simply don't need on a trip. Luckily, I then found busuu. First, you do a test that lets you start learning at exactly your Spanish level (after Duolingo I wasn't a complete beginner anymore), and the way it's set up makes the words and grammar sink in. I quickly became a fan and bought the premium program to access all the classes. This is a lot cheaper than taking a Spanish course and you can study while being on a plane or bus. I soon could follow conversations between locals. Speaking myself is still difficult but it's nice to see that I am making progress every day.
Another good app to learn Spanish easily and playfully is the free Babel Spanish app.

Tips on how to find cheap flights to Spain (and to any other country for that matter)

When you are in Europe, it's incredible how cheaply you can fly to Madrid or Barcelona. So cheap in fact, that you can easily go for a weekend trip. Of course, that still depends on the dates and doesn't work during the main holidays. With the following tips, you should be able to find cheap flights to Spain even if you arrive from overseas or can only travel during the official summer holidays.

1. Use several flight search engines

I usually start looking for flights on **Skyscanner** and then I compare the deals from there with **CheapTickets** and/or **Opodo**. These sites tend to have the cheapest prices. Skyscanner for example, lets you set a price alert which will inform you with an e-mail when they have cheaper flights. You could do that half a year before your trip. Another possibility is to type your flight into Google directly to get an estimate of how much the airfare will be. In the end, I always check on the websites of the cheapest airlines directly. For Europe it's EasyJet and Ryanair.

2. Be early and buy your flight at least 3 months in advance

If you know the dates of your vacation, there is no use to wait with booking your flights. They will only get more expensive.

On the other hand: In times of covid, you should plan all your travel last-minute. Once you are sure that the country you want to visit is open and it will be agreeable to travel under the current circumstances.

3. Be slightly flexible

Check the dates three days prior and after the dates you chose to fly. There might be a difference up to $300! If you search with CheapTickets or Skyscanner it's very easy to have an overview of the flight prices on different dates.

4. Travel from other airports and book multi-leg flights

Especially if you travel from Europe, it makes sense to check the airports in the surrounding countries and then buy a connecting flight from your country to get there (or better a train ride). The cheaper airports to fly from are London, Munich, Frankfurt am Main, Düsseldorf, Basel, Paris, Milan, Amsterdam, and Brussels.

So, yes, if you have enough time, it's sometimes worth it to travel in several legs. If you fly from the US, often New York and Philadelphia are the cheapest. Just calculate enough time in your connecting airport in case your first plane is delayed because you will have to go get your luggage and check it in for your new flight.

However: In times of covid, you should opt for a direct flight, since every additional stop can mean more tests, more regulations, and a possible quarantine.

5. Delete your browser history

The websites where you searched for your flight tickets to Spain will recognize you on your second visit and raise the prices a little since you are still interested. So, if you notice an increase in the price, the first thing to do is to close the website, clear the browser history and then start searching again once you are ready to book. It's astounding, how quickly you can save money this way.

6. Sign up for the newsletter from your favorite airlines

Newsletters still offer good value and often you find cheap airfares in them. At the moment, I regularly receive special offers from TUI and Iberia. By the way, SwissMissOnTour.com offers a newsletter as well. Sign up on the website to receive my latest blog posts and a free and helpful packing list.

7. Flying cheap within Spain

Luckily, flights within Spain generally are cheap. If you book up to three weeks before you travel, the flight tickets might be even cheaper than what the bus or train ticket would cost. However, think about it whether the time you save is worth the damage to the environment.

Important Spanish festivals and traditions

Spain has a few festivals that are known all around the world. Perhaps because they are a bit controversial, like the running of the bulls in Pamplona or La Tomatina where people get into huge tomato throwing street fights. The fun of the latter also attracts tourists from around the world but it's surprising that the rest of the equally great festivals in Spain aren't just as famous. At lots of those festivals, you will also be able to see the traditional Flamenco dances and costumes. But let's look at the Spanish festivities in more detail.

La Tomatina

This festival takes place in Buñol on the last Wednesday in August every year. It's the closest that Europe gets to an Indian Holi festival, but instead of throwing colors, people throw tomatoes at each other. Best wear closed shoes and swimming goggles. Also, since 2013 the festival is limited to 20'000 visitors, and you need to buy a ticket. I didn't find the official ticket page of the municipality, however, on this website, the packages have a good value: https://ticketstomatina.com.

San Fermin – Running with the bulls

This festival takes place yearly for 7 days at the beginning of July in Pamplona. Every morning, a group of bulls will chase anyone willing to run through the streets. It's a Spanish tradition, but I wouldn't recommend it since bulls as well as people get hurt. You can find more information on this website: https://www.sanfermin.com/en/running-of-the-bulls/quick-guide-what-is-the-running-of-the-bulls/

La Tamborrada

This festival is celebrated in San Sebastian in January when for 24 hours the streets are filled with parades of drumming people. It's fun to watch or if you have your own drum, you can join some public drumming events.

Flamenco

Flamenco is a Spanish dance and folkloric music where the dancers and musicians want to express emotions and soul. The women wear beautiful, layered dresses, and the dance moves are accompanied by feet stomping, clapping, fan art, and playing castanets.

La Semana Santa

Holy Week takes place in many Spanish cities in the week leading up to Easter. So, usually in April. It's probably the most important festival in Spain. Parades are held with religiously decorated floats. During this time, it's hard to find accommodation.

Different Spanish Fairs

There are several great fairs taking place in major Spanish cities during Summer. You will be able to stroll through booths, sit down in tents to drink and eat, watch concerts, Flamenco shows, or bullfights. Usually, men and women wear traditional Flamenco clothes even if they are just visitors to the festival and the whole fairgrounds are beautifully decorated with many lights. The biggest fairs are the Feria de Abril in Seville (in April), in Cordoba at the end of May, in Marbella in June, and in Malaga in August.

Traveling by train and bus – public transport in Spain

In Spain, it's very easy to travel by train or bus since there are good connections between all the tourist spots. To look up the different options and schedules, I simply type my starting point and destination on one of the following websites:

- https://omio.com/
- https://www.thetrainline.com/

You will enjoy looking out of the window, marveling at the sea, vineyards, and big fields or mountain ranges, without having to worry about concentrating on the road.

The Spanish train company is called **Renfe,** and my train usually was punctual by the minute. Of course, you can also purchase your train ticket on their website directly.

There are many different bus companies such as **Avanza** or **Alsa**.

Although some journeys might seem to have steep prices at first glance, if you compare it with the fuel price and the price of parking spots in Spain, you will save a lot of money by traveling by public transport instead of by rental car.

Renting a car in Spain

Traveling by car is very convenient, especially if you drive along the north coast. Then, you can stop at any secluded beach, grab your surfboard, and head into the ocean. Also, in all the other urban regions of Spain, a rental car gives you the freedom to leave or arrive whenever you want. In addition, most of the roads in Spain (except in the city centers) were relatively empty and driving was pleasant.

The downside is that gas isn't cheap and parking lots are expensive as well. Therefore, I researched free parking in Spain. I noted some of the locations that I found but I never felt entirely comfortable just abandoning my car in some suburban street. Surely always take all your belongings with you, so that the car looks empty and not worth being broken into.

On white parking spaces, you could mostly park for free. On the blue parking spaces, there was an ATM somewhere along this road that you had to feed with coins or a credit card. Either you typed in your license plate number, or you got a ticket that you put behind the windshield. In the blue fields, you usually only had to pay between 9 a.m. and 2 p.m. and 4 p.m. and 9 p.m. If you are unsure somewhere, you better ask a local nearby for advice. Often a policeman will be passing by anyway, handing out fines, because they circulate all the time in Spain. So don't think that you can leave your car for 5 minutes.

If you want to park your car in a parking garage, 24h in a public parking garage will cost between 14 and 20 EUR. In hotels between 18 and 25 EUR. Parking garages have the advantage that no passers-by or other drivers would damage your car. Many cars in Spain have dents and are in bad condition, mainly due to the narrow parking spaces in side streets and the narrow alleys in the city centers. We have also seen someone touch another car while rolling backward out of a parking space.

In addition, I find driving in Spanish cities complicated. They have roundabouts with traffic lights, and you always have to pay extra attention in order not to accidentally run a red light or land in the wrong lane.

The cheapest place to rent a car is Madrid. It might be cheaper to rent it there and drive to Andalusia with visiting some nice places along the way, than simply renting it in Seville or Malaga.

I rented my car with www.doyouspain.com because they had the cheapest prices. The first time I wanted to come to Spain, I actually had covid and couldn't start my trip. DoYouSpain

was very generous and just refunded me the money, although it said in my booking that it was non-refundable. On my next visit, I rented the car through DoYouSpain with Goldcar at Malaga airport (it was only a third as expensive as if I had gotten the car in town). All in all, our trip would certainly have been poss-ible without a car, but just for the spectacular road trip between Ronda and Marbella, the rental was worth it.

Overview of the distances and driving times in Andalusia

Start	Destination	Distance and Time
Madrid	Granada	419 km, 4h
Granada	Malaga	124 km, 1h35
Malaga	Marbella	60 km, 50 mins
Malaga	Gibraltar	136 km, 1h45

Malaga	Cordoba	158 km, 1h45
Malaga	Ronda	103 km, 1h20
Ronda	Cadiz	144 km, 1h40
Cadiz	Seville	121 km, 1h15
Seville	Cordoba	143 km, 1h35
Cordoba	Madrid	404 km, 4h

Traveling in Spain with children

Europeans often choose Spain as their first destination to travel to with kids. Reasons for that are the many wide, flat, golden, safe beaches. On top of that, you will find a lot of playgrounds that you wished you had access to when you were a child yourself. Kids definitely will have fun in Spain. In addition, there are many nice cafés where you can take a break. Most of the time there are enough baby chairs in the restaurants. Also, it is no problem to get a baby seat with your rental car or bike.

In the supermarkets like Carrefour, Mercadona, and Aldi you can find powdered milk and baby food from Nestlé and some other brands as well as their own brands of diapers and baby food. So, you will find something to provide for the basic needs of your toddler. However, my daughter didn't like the Spanish baby food and we looked for Pampers in vain. If your baby is fussy about diapers or food, you should take them with you for the whole trip. Fortunately, it was no problem for us to simply switch to the various fruits and give her unsalted potatoes or soft vegetables at the restaurants.

Now let's take a look at some more tips that will make a trip to Andalusia a pleasure for everyone involved.

1. Plan generous time frames

With kids, you need to plan generous time slots for everything when planning your trip. Then your visit will be stress-free, and you won't be disappointed because the tour of the fourth museum didn't fit into the day's schedule after all. Better stay an extra day in Spain.

2. Take more breaks

Whether you sit down in a café or an ice cream parlor and everyone gets to choose something, or you stop at a playground in a park somewhere, it's worth recharging both your batteries and the kids' every now and then. Sometimes it's necessary to retreat to your hotel room for an hour and just enjoy the quiet. Don't think of it as lost time, but as a helpful oasis of calm so that your child doesn't whine afterward as you stroll around the city for several hours.

3. Bring enough snacks and drinks with you

On a trip, it's easy to get hungry or thirsty and there's no open restaurant or supermarket nearby. Hunger or thirst can even turn adults into angry animals, so you should never let your child get into this situation. Be sure to include some snacks and plenty of water, unsweetened tea, or syrup in your daypack.

4. Let the children participate

Children love to discover and learn things. For example, give them the task of reading the map or planning an activity so they can actively participate in the travel process.

5. Plan an activity each day that is especially fun for the children

This could be letting them bounce around on the big hotel bed before sightseeing or letting your baby crawl down the hotel hallway and spreading some objects along the way for it to investigate. The following six suggestions are a selection that can be used as program points with children in Andalusia.

- Visit the Bioparc in Fuengirola (www.bioparcfuengirola.es): At this unique zoo, you can get up close to some of the world's most exotic animals, including gorillas, lemurs and crocodiles.
- Go to the beach on the Costa del Sol: The warm sandy beaches on the Costa del Sol are ideal for families to relax and play in the sun.
- Stay at a hotel with a kids club: many all-inclusive hotels offer fun childcare. At the great Kids Club at Marbella Club Hotel, you can also pay to put your kids in care for one or more days even if you're not staying there (www.marbellaclub.com/kids-club).
- Stop at one of the many playgrounds: Spain has nice playgrounds everywhere, both in the city centers and on the beaches. Unfortunately, there is often little shade, but you can plan your visit for the morning or late afternoon.
- Explore the caves of Nerja (www.cuevadenerja.es/): The underground world of the Caves of Nerja, with its stalactites, stalagmites, and ancient cave paintings, is sure to fascinate children.

- Take a horse-drawn carriage ride in Cordoba or Seville: kids will love seeing the city's famous sights from a traditional horse-drawn carriage.

6. Bring a baby carrier

Especially because there often are narrow and steep cobblestone streets in Andalusia, it is an advantage to have a sling or baby carrier with you. This way you can carry the baby or child on your body in a way that is easy on the back and also gives the child an extra portion of closeness, which probably leads to a better mood for the child.

We started with a towel wrap, which is very practical because you can tie the baby to your body in all sorts of ways. Also, you can make sure that the sling is made of natural fibers and the baby has enough air to breathe or the head is supported. The disadvantages I find is that the cloth is so long and sometimes drags along the floor when you tie it. Also, when rolled up, it is still as big as a small sleeping bag, which already takes up a considerable amount of space in the backpack. Therefore, much more suitable for traveling is a backpack-like carrier with less fabric and you can choose whether you want to wear it in the front or on the back. For traveling and hiking we now only use this carrier, because it is much more space-saving, and you can carry toddlers up to 3 years old like in a backpack or fanny pack. Especially for visiting the Alhambra in Granada, a baby carrier is necessary as strollers are prohibited in many areas and our visit lasted over three hours.

7. Tips for arriving by plane

If you are traveling by plane, you don't need to worry. So far, I have found the airport staff to be very helpful with anything related to children or babies. Sometimes there are special family check-in counters where you don't have to wait in line as much. If you have a stroller that is made up of several separate pieces, you can check it in for free. Or instead of the stroller, you can check in an infant carrier for free. If your stroller is only one piece, you will get a label code for it at check-in and then be allowed to take the stroller to the gate. It must simply fit through the security scanner when folded. Just before you board the plane, you give the folded stroller to the staff. Either you get it back when you get off the plane or it comes on the baggage carousel. I have experienced both.

There are also special conditions for baby food. You can take glasses with baby food and milk in containers larger than 100ml. You just have to put them in a zipped plastic bag on the security belt. Normally they scan the food with an extra device until you are allowed to take it back. Usually, you can take up to 1 liter of liquids/foods.
Even when I was traveling in London without a child and still wanted to take the pumped milk home, it was no problem. I just put the milk containers on the conveyor along with the breast pump. Even though the staff was male, no questions were asked, and they simply screened the milk again before letting me have it. So, you don't have to worry about that, at least in Europe. The staff is well trained and since they are aware of how important breast milk is for the baby, you can take breast milk on the plane without a baby as well as with the baby.

8. Tips if you travel pregnant

Maybe until now you have always been traveling as a backpacker and have been staying in shared rooms. Soon you will share your room and your life with a new person. That's why, especially during pregnancy, it's the perfect time to treat yourself to another trip to the beach or a beautiful city where you can really pamper yourself. Take a nice hotel room with a private bathroom, because you will probably have to go to the bathroom more often and you might feel nauseous sometimes. What always helped me against nausea was that I never had an empty stomach. If I always had some kind of snack handy (preferably something bland, like rusks or some bread) and ate that as soon as I had the slightest hint of nausea, the nausea was gone.

Once again, enjoy sleeping in a big bed and using all the pillows to be comfortable even with your big belly.

Don't plan too much. You need energy for two now. Therefore, walk or ride around the city only as long as you feel fit. Sleep longer in the morning or go to bed earlier, whatever feels good. Drink more water than usual, wear support stockings (against dizzy spells and varicose veins) and take breaks to rest your feet either in your hotel room or in one of the many beautiful parks in Andalusia. Don't eat oysters or other delicate, raw foods, and don't drink cava until after the birth, but enjoy all the other delicacies Andalusia has to offer. You can eat well in Spain even if you are pregnant.

Finally, you should take your mommy passport with you, which contains information about all previous checkups and your blood type. Most likely, you will spend your vacation in Andalusia without any incidents and it will be over much too quickly. But if anything happens, at least you can go to the hospital well prepared. For all other questions you can talk to your gynecologist in advance.

Most airlines will take a pregnant woman until the 37th week.

Typical Spanish food and drinks

I am sure you know about Sangria, Spanish olives, and Spanish ham and have heard of tapas. But what exactly are tapas? Plus, there are so many more delicacies in Spain that are worth trying, so let's have a look at what you need to eat and drink while you are in Andalusia.

- **Tapas**

Tapas can be anything that is a small snack. It probably started with olives and Spanish ham that you receive free on your table when drinking a beer or glass of wine. However, if you enjoy a beer or wine during tapas hour today, you are in for a variety of choices. Accompanied with your drink whose prices can start as low as 99c you can usually check what tapas are displayed on the bar and pick whichever attracts you most. It could be fried potato balls or fish cakes, small sandwiches with ham, anchovies, tomato spread, shrimp cocktail, or anything you can think of. Hence, it's worth trying many different tapas bars with their individual creations. In restaurants you order tapas from the menu and the drink you usually have to order extra. At markets, you can also buy various tapas but mostly you pay 1-3 EUR for each piece.

Instead of tapas, you might also read *Pintxos*. Those are tapas that originated in the Basque region. Often, they are more sophisticated or extravagant tapas.

- **Gazpacho or Salmorejo**

This dish actually originated in Andalusia. It is a cold tomato soup mixed with cucumbers and bell peppers. Further, it contains olive oil, croutons (breadcrumbs), garlic, and basil. The flavor is delicious so that you might wonder why you've ever eaten soup hot before. On top of that, it's healthy and perfect to cool down on hot days. Salmorejo has nothing to do with salmon (except perhaps the orange color) but is a thicker version of gazpacho to which ham and egg are added. Salmorejo actually comes from Córdoba, but it can be found all over Andalusia.

- **Paella**

This is a perfect dish for festivals since it usually is cooked in huge pans where fried rice is mixed with vegetables and chicken or seafood. Typically, it's decorated with big prawns that you can enjoy when you manage to peel them out of their shell. You will find differently flavored Paellas all over Spain, but it's always based on the same original dish.

- **Cava**

Cava is a Spanish type of sparkling wine. It is mostly produced in Catalonia. The refreshing bubbles are perfect when you enjoy a beautiful sunset somewhere.

- **Sangria**

This is light red wine (or, more recently, often also white wine) that is enriched with fresh fruit like pineapple, grapes, melon, orange, or apple. This gives the wine an additional fruity flavor and people enjoy drinking it out of 1-liter jars that they share with their friends or partner.

- **Jamon Iberico and Jamon Serrano**

You might eat this as part of tapas or find the delicious ham on your breakfast table. The difference is that Jamon Iberico is considered a delicacy that is quite expensive because it's made of only one pig species in a certain region. It is darker than Jamon Serrano and richer in flavor. Jamon Serrano originated in the Andalusian mountain ranges but there are fewer restrictions on how it needs to be produced. Therefore, it's cheaper but still delicious if you like dried ham.

- **Bocadillo**

That's the Spanish word for sandwich. They are practical if you go on a hike or are busy sightseeing and don't have time to sit down in a restaurant. Often, bocadillos are filled with only one ingredient but all the more of that. Therefore, you can have very juicy ham sandwiches.

- **Gambas al Ajillo**

This dish is served in a sizzling hot clay pan. It consists of shrimp that are deep-fried in hot oil with chili and garlic. Sometimes, the sauce also contains a tomato flavor. You eat it with white bread that you dip in the oil and on which you scoop up the shrimp and garlic. It's best eaten at the beach, but you can find this dish in almost any restaurant in Spain since it's a favorite amongst tourists.

- **Churros with chocolate**

Churros are rolls out of deep-fried dough covered in sugar and a sauce. With my sweet tooth, my love for churros is obvious. Regarding chocolate, I am a harsh critic since we have such delicious chocolate in Switzerland. However, in Spain, you can also find amazing liquid chocolate. It's thick and rich and a perfect combination to dip your churros. In each town, you will find at least one famous churreria. You recognize the best ones on the queue that is lined up in front of the restaurant. It's worth the wait or coming back for a reserved table! The drinking chocolate is also good as an energy boost without the churros.

Sometimes, the churros aren't long but round, like donuts. They are just as delicious since they are even puffier and not so dense.

Two-week itinerary to see the best of culture and nature

Your journey begins in the lively coastal city of Malaga, where sunshine and the Spanish cuisine await you. From here, you'll be taken on an adventure through the stunning landscapes, rich history, and warm culture of Andalusia. The route will take you through breathtaking cities like Granada, famous for the magnificent Alhambra, as well as Seville, the amazing capital of Andalusia. You will experience the unique culture of Cordoba and visit the white buildings in Cadiz. Since it is a round trip, you can start or end the trip anywhere in Andalusia, depending on where the cheapest flight brings you to.

If you still have time at the beginning or at the end and want to experience the travel magic further, you should enrich your trip with an extension to Madrid

Day 1: Arrival in Malaga

 Arrive in this lively coastal city and get a taste of the sea air. Stroll along the harbor and beach promenade and enjoy your first glass of cava, sangria, and tapas. Take a walk through the historic center and visit the most important sights, for example the cathedral or the birthplace of Picasso.

Day 2: Malaga

 Today, choose between visiting ancient architecture by climbing the hilltop castle, relaxing in the botanical gardens or on the beach, or visiting the Picasso Museum or the Carmen Thyssen Museum. Of course, you could also go shopping in Spain's great clothing stores.

Day 3: A spectacular hike

If you are up for an adventure, reserve your time slot for today to do the hike at Caminito del Rey. In case you don't want to get too sweaty but still would like to see more of Spain's nature, head to El Torcal de Antequera.

Day 4: Granada

 Head to Granada. Stroll through the Alhambra (note: tickets must be pre-booked online) and enjoy the beautiful architecture and fruity scents of the garden. Be sure to plan enough time to visit

this sprawling castle complex. Since the old town is also very pretty, be sure to stroll around in the evening or the next morning.

Day 5: Granada

Your legs are probably still a bit tired from yesterday's visit to the Alhambra. Nevertheless, today you should take a look at the remaining part of the historic city center that you didn't see yesterday. The cathedral with the Arabic souk or the white cave houses in Sacormonte are worth visiting. Drive to Marbella in the afternoon.

Day 6: Marbella

It's time for the beach and some quality holiday time again. Take a walk along the promenade and through the pretty, historical town center.

Day 7: Ronda

Take a day trip from Marbella. The road between Marbella and Ronda opens up spectacular views. Marvel at this architectural masterpiece and swim in pristine natural pools. Perhaps, taste some wine in one of the nearby wineries.

Day 8: Gibraltar

Enter this country for one day and climb or ride up to the top of the rock. Enjoy the amazing view across the meeting point of the

Mediterranean Sea and the Atlantic Ocean and spot some wild monkeys.

Day 9: Cadiz

Take pictures of the pretty white town and relax or surf at the beach.

Day 10: Seville

Wow, it's quite a change of pace after all the small towns you have visited and now suddenly you are in the capital of Andalusia. There is so much you could do. Head to the Metropol Parasol to enjoy the view, watch a Flamenco show if you haven't done so yet, and start a walk through the historic city center.

Day 11: Seville

Continue your walk to see Seville's best sights. Be sure to stop by the cathedral, Plaza de España, and the Real Alcázar. Also head across the river and fill your belly at Triana market.

Day 12: Seville

Book a tour of the roof of the cathedral. Visit the Archivo de Indias, a UNESCO World Heritage Site that houses an impressive collection of documents on the history of the Americas. Stroll through the Jewish neighborhood of Santa Cruz and settle into a restaurant in one of the narrow streets.

Day 13: Cordoba

Walk through the Jewish quarter and marvel at the colorful houses. Walk across the roman bridge and relax in the beautiful courtyards.

Day 14: Departure from Madrid, Malaga, or Seville

From Cordoba, it's easy to reach either of the three bigger cities with international airports. So, head to the one that is most convenient for you, in order to get back to your home.

In Madrid you could visit an art museum and relax in Parque Retiro.

Enjoy one last drink with some tapas or a hot chocolate and churros before you leave.

This is a possible two-week trip how you could manage to see all the highlights in Andalusia. Now, let's look at the individual places in a bit more detail.

Malaga

When hearing Malaga, probably, Picasso, sunshine, and a picturesque town by the sea come to your mind. That's all true and hence, Malaga really offers a great combination for a perfect summer holiday by the beach. Apart from the lively and pretty port and being the birth town of the famous painter Pablo Picasso, there also is Moorish and Roman history, and so much to see in the surrounding area, that you can easily base yourself for a week or longer just in Malaga.

In order to visit a nature park, to do a hike, having a rental car is convenient. It's a very popular city to rent a car and therefore, you have many options. Nevertheless, you should pre-book your car well in advance to have cheaper options and it's still more expensive than if you rent a car in Madrid. That being said, let's look at what to do within the city of Malaga first.

How to get to Malaga

Malaga has an international airport and so you can start your adventure directly in Malaga when coming from your home. The cheapest and quickest way into the city center is by train, which takes less than 15 minutes and only costs 1.80 EUR. A taxi will cost 20-25 EUR for the 12 km.

By bus, you can reach Malaga from Granada in 2.5 hours with hourly connections. From Cordoba, it takes about 1 hour by train or 2.5 hours by bus (a bit cheaper). From Seville, it takes 2 to 3 hours by train or 2.5 to 5 hours by bus, even though on the map it looks like Seville is really far away. So, actually, it's very easy to travel between the bigger cities in Andalusia by public transport.

If you come by car, you can check for free parking spots in the area around *C. Conde de Ureña*, since you might get lucky there.

A ride with the local bus within Malaga costs 1.30 EUR and gets cheaper if you purchase a bus card for Malaga.

What to do in Malaga

Situated at the Costa del Sol (sunny coast), it's obvious that you must spend some time at the beach. But of course, you don't want to miss out on the rich culture either.

Visit the Picasso Museum

Since Picasso was born in Malaga, this museum has the biggest collection of the famous Spanish painter. Even if you aren't an art fan, this museum would be a great opportunity to be inspired by colors, structures, and emotions that paintings can create and to learn about his life.

The entrance fee is 9 EUR but it's free in the last two visiting hours on Sundays (get there right at the beginning) or on 28. February (Andalusia Day), 18. May (International Museum Day), and 27. September (World Tourism Day).

If you have an ID that shows that you are a teacher, it's free as well.

You can pre-book the tickets online and check the daily opening times since they change every season (www.museopicassomalaga.org/ en/hours-admission). The museum is open every day from 10 a.m.

If you want to see the house where Picasso grew up, you have to go to *Pl. de la Merced, 15*. The entry fee to the Casa Natal is 3 EUR for the living quarters and a combined ticket of 4 EUR to see a small collection of paintings as well. The museum is open every day from 9.30 a.m. to 8 p.m. and if you can show that you study fine arts or are a teacher, the visit is free.

Visit another museum

There is a big variety of great museums in Malaga. A gallery, that you must see, if just from the outside, is the **Centre Pompidou**. It's a sister of the original one in Paris and it's housed in a colorful cube. Here, you will see modern art and often there is art by very famous artists. The museum is closed on Tuesdays and otherwise open from 9.30 a.m. to 8 p.m. every day. It costs 9 EUR to see everything or 4 EUR if you only want to see the temporary exhibition. It's free on Sundays from 4 p.m. until the end or always if you are an art student or teacher.

My second choice would be the **Carmen Thyssen Museum**, of which you can find another collection in Madrid. It showcases works by Spanish painters in various styles. The entry fee is 10 EUR or 6 EUR if you can get a reduced ticket. The museum is open every day from 10 a.m. to 8 p.m.

If you like history, you should visit the biggest museum in Andalusia; **Museo de Malaga**. It's a history and archeology museum and shows some fine art as well. So, something for everyone. The best thing is it only costs 1.50 EUR to enter and is free for EU citizens. It's closed on Mondays, otherwise open from 9 a.m. to 8 p.m. except on Sundays, when it's open from 9 a.m. to 3 p.m.

A fun museum is the small **wine museum**. Of course, wine is a big part of Spain, and therefore, a visit to this museum in Malaga makes sense. The entry price is 5 EUR or 3 EUR if you are a student. You get to sample two glasses of wine. Any additional sample is 1 EUR. Address: Plaza de la Aduana, opening hours: Monday to Friday: 10 a.m. to 5 p.m. and Saturdays until 2 p.m.

If you are in Malaga for a longer amount of time, you should also visit **The Malaga Automobile and Fashion Museum**. The owners were probably thinking; hm, how can we create a museum that will attract men and women at the same time? The exhibition shows beautiful, luxurious cars and high fashion dresses, and they succeeded in creating interesting showrooms. It's open every day from 10 a.m. to 7 p.m. and costs 9.50 EUR.

Relax at the best beaches

After so much time in museums, at last, you should head to the beach. The closest beach to the city center and therefore a good answer if you don't have much time and just want to get to the water is **Playa de la Malagueta**. It's busy with tourists, and locals and lined with bars and restaurants, so it's easy to have a good time by the water.

A better option, if you have some time, is to rent a bike and cycle to **Playa De El Palo**. The bike ride takes 15 minutes, and you will pass several other beaches along the way. Hence, you can stop wherever you want. It's also possible to walk the 5 km in about one hour or take bus 3 or 11 directly to Playa De El Palo from Plaza de Toros. This beach has a more local feel to it. The sand is very flat, and the water is safe to enter. The best thing along those local

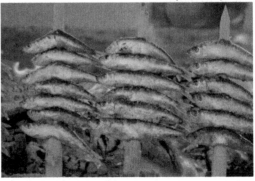

46

beaches are the cooked *Espetos* that you can buy and eat. They are freshly caught sardines that are roasted above embers on old boats on the sand. It's a Malaga specialty and you should try it.

A pretty beach without restaurant facilities and, therefore, more natural (nevertheless populated on weekends) is **Playa Peñón Del Cuervo,** which is 7.5 km from the city center and easily reachable by bicycle. All in all, Malaga is a very bike-friendly city with lots of cycling paths.

Enjoy the port area

For sunset drinks, take a walk in the pretty port area. It's lined with palm trees, fountains, restaurants, bars, and modern souvenir shops. You definitely won't be bored while you have the picturesque view of the water and the ships as an additional benefit.

Be impressed by ancient architecture

Of course, you have long seen the two forts towering above the city. First, let's visit the Moorish **Alcazaba** palace since it's located right behind the Malaga Museum and the University of Malaga. It's much smaller than the Alhambra in Granada but actually less crowded and nice to visit. When going back down, you can walk past a well-preserved Roman open-air theater. This is free to visit, and I thought it amazing to find such a beautiful location of Roman heritage in Spain.

The second monument is the **Castillo de Gibralfaro** which can be reached from the city center in a 20 minutes' walk. You have access to the castle wall from where you have a great view of the city and the bullfighting arena.

Both the Alcazaba and Castillo de Gibralfaro are open from 9 a.m. to 8 p.m. from 1. April to 31. October and from 9 a.m. to 6 p.m. during the rest of the year. On Sundays from 2 p.m. to closing the entrance is free. Otherwise, it costs 3.50 EUR per monument or 5.50 with the combined ticket. We enjoyed our visit to the Castillo de Gibralfaro and were surprised at how large and expansive the castle grounds were.

One more monument that you need to see in Malaga is the **cathedral**. It looks beautiful from the outside even though it only has one tower although it initially was planned to have two towers. That's why the cathedral is lovingly nicknamed "the one-armed woman". The cathedral is richly decorated inside and, therefore, you might be interested in paying 6 EUR for the visit. However, you will have an even more special visit, if you purchase a ticket to the roof of the cathedral, which has a pretty structure, and you get a great view of the city. A combined ticket costs 10 EUR. Only access to the roof is 6 EUR. Roof access after dark is 10 EUR. It's open Monday to Saturday from 10 a.m. to 6 p.m. and 2 p.m. to 6 p.m. on Sundays.

Discover street art

If you like street art, take a walk in the SOHO area. There are various huge and colorful murals on the buildings. For example, along *Calle San Lorenzo*.

Take a breather in Parque de Malaga

Whenever you feel tired, head to a bench inside the park of Malaga and simply enjoy this green island. You will see many exotic plants, nice palm trees, sculptures, and fountains.

Dive into another world in the botanical gardens

The botanical gardens of Malaga are situated 8 km outside the city center but well worth a trip by bus. There is a nice bamboo forest and many different flowers and trees. Normally, the entrance fee is 5.20 EUR but free on Sundays from 9.30 a.m. - 4.30 p.m. from October to March and between 3.30 p.m. and 7.30 p.m. from April to September. You can stay in the gardens for up to 90 minutes after closing time. Get there by bus number 2 from *Alameda Principal* and get off at the last stop. The bus runs every 15 minutes. You will then have to walk for about 15 minutes. From the main bus station, bus number 91 drives directly to the gardens. However, it only leaves every 90 minutes.

Fill your stomach in Atarazanas Market

The Mercado Central Atara-zanas is located in a beautiful steel and glass building with painted windows. Hence, the building on its own is worth a visit but I am sure you won't leave without having sampled at least some kind of fruit or olive or bought a freshly made drink. The mar-ket is open from Monday to Saturday, from 8 a.m. until the vendors are sold out around 2 or 3 p.m. It is closed on Sundays.

Day trips from Malaga

Malaga is a good base to do hikes in the surrounding areas or to visit another pretty city along the coast. Of course, you can also spend a night or two in those cities, without returning to Malaga.

Take a hike in El Torcal de Antequera

The Torcal de Antequera Natural Park attracts hikers with green pastures and incredible karst rock formations. If you are lucky, you might also spot animals such as badgers, weasels, ibex, or snakes. It's a pretty scenery and very easily accessible by car since it's only 50 km from Malaga and there is free parking available at the start of the trails. If the parking lot is full, there is a second parking lot from which you can take a shuttle bus for 1.50 EUR to the start of the trails. However, since the trails are quite short, you can also walk the distance. Entry to El Torcal is free.

In case you want to come by public transport, it's a bit more complicated since there is no bus going to the nature park. Hence, you need to take a train or bus from Malaga to Antequera (approx. 1 hour) and there, haggle with a taxi. A taxi that shuttles you there and back and will wait for one hour will ask for about 40 EUR.

Two trails are open to the public. The green trail is 1.5 km, and you will need about 45 minutes for the round trip.

The yellow trail measures 2.8 km and you will need about 2 hours for the round trip.

Both hikes are easy, however, there are some steep ascends and the terrain might get slippery. Hence, it's important that you wear shoes with a good profile. Also, you should stick to the trails and only do the hike when the sky is clear of clouds since it could get foggy quickly and it's easy to lose orientation between the rocks and get lost. However, the trails are clearly marked. One more tip: Bring a windbreaker jacket since temperatures can drop significantly compared to Malaga. Here you are at an altitude of about 1200 m.

After the park, you can stop in Antequera for something to eat. There is free parking along *Camino de la Moraleda.* Antequera is a pretty town with a nice church and lots of picturesque, white buildings.

Dare to enter El Caminito del Rey

This hike was said to be the most dangerous hike in Europe. However, this was before the trails were renovated and secured. While you still have steep drops next to you the whole way, it's all secured by fences now. In case heights don't give you vertigo, El Caminito del Rey will fill your holiday with an amazing adventure full of spectacular views. You will remember them a long time after having been there. Also keep an eye out for vultures along the hike. We saw several ones of them spreading their wide wings.

El Caminito del Rey by car

The entry point to El Caminito del Rey is the restaurant **El Kiosko**. By car, you can reach it from Malaga in 1 hour by taking the A-357 heading toward Campillos. At Ardales you take a right onto MA-5403 until you reach the restaurant.

El Caminito del Rey by public transport

By public transport, you take a train from Malaga to *El Chorro-Alora* which takes about 50 minutes. From there, you need to take the shuttle bus to El Kiosko for 1.50 EUR. The ending point of the hike is at El Chorro train station again and so you can take the train directly back from there, without having to go to El Kiosko. Unfortunately, there are only about two train departures every day. Therefore, you have to book your hike well in advance, in order to be able to book a time slot that fits your train schedule. You should arrive at El Chorro train station about 2 hours before the hike. This will give you enough time to take the shuttle bus to El Kiosko and then hike the 20 minutes to the entry gate. Once you enter the entry gate, the actual hike only takes 1.5 to 2 hours.

Book your hiking spot in advance

This is a big tourist attraction, and you need to pre-book tickets online, a few weeks in advance (www.caminitodelrey.info/es/entradas/comprar).
On their website, you can even take a virtual tour.
It costs 10 EUR to do the hike including a rental helmet. It's worth it to pay the extra 1.50 EUR to be able to take a shuttle bus from the end of the hike back to the parking lot. You can do the hike in only one direction and otherwise would need to find your own way back through the gorge which would be at least another 8 km. So, after already having completed El Caminito del Rey you can really reward yourself by riding back on the shuttle bus.

Wear good shoes and comfortable clothes. Hiking poles and big backpacks are forbidden.

The order of the hike

Be aware that El Kiosko is not the start of the hike. 200 m from the restaurant back along the road, you need to access a tunnel and walk 20 minutes (1.5 km) to the entry gate (15 minutes if you walk quickly). At first, it's a little uphill and after that downhill again. You have to be at the entry gate 30 minutes before the time your hike starts. There, you will receive a helmet and they will check your footwear and whether you brought any forbidden objects like selfie-sticks. They are very strict and take the protection of the gorge serious. So, read the rules when you buy the ticket, in order not to be disappointed.

Then, you can start the 7.7 km hike with the other people from your time slot. However, you can walk at your own pace. Take in the picturesque views. A big part of the hike also leads through a normal pine forest, where you have shade from the sun and can take a break.
Once the trail is finished, you have to walk 2 more kilometers to get to the town of El Chorro, where you will hand back your helmet. Then, it's another 5 minutes to reach the train station (past all the tour busses) from where you can take the shuttle bus back to the parking lot at El Kiosko (or the train back to Malaga).

My tour with Visitanddo Andalusia

Since I was too late to get a time slot that would have worked out with the train schedule, I was very glad that I could book a tour to Caminito del Rey with Visitanddo.com.

They picked me up at my hotel in the morning. Already during the bus ride, our great guide Shirley told us many stories about the area and the hike. After a quick stop in the beautiful white village of Ardales, we arrived at the starting point of the Hike at El Kiosko. 20 minutes and one tunnel crossing plus many stunning lake views later, we reached the entry area where we were handed a mandatory helmet.

A knowledgeable guide was included in the tour price and we learned many interesting facts along the route but you could also choose to walk on your own at your preferred speed. The hike through the gorge only takes about 1.5 hours and isn't really physically challenging. The only things that take your breath away are the stunning views across the gorge and the milky green water. And perhaps the heat or winds can be tough on your body. In the end, I nevertheless was glad to reach the finishing point, where I handed back my helmet and then had the opportunity to buy ice cream at one of the cute stands at the picnic area there. The price of the food and fresh fruit juices they offered was very fair and hence, you don't necessarily need to bring a lot of snacks on your hike.

Afterward, it was nice to just lean back on our comfortable bus and be transported back to the hotel in Malaga.

If you'd like to book a trip to Caminito del Rey with Visitanddo you can do it through the following link:
www.visitanddo.com/en/agents/?ttafid=24631.

Granada

This is the city where the different cultural influences of Andalusia are most visible. Within Granada's walkable city center, you find Arab baths and markets, Moorish castles, and Spanish tapas or Flamenco bars. There is a beautiful ancient building or structure at every corner and in the background, you see the powdery white Sierra Nevada mountains. In winter, you can go skiing there and in the rest of the year, you find beautiful hiking paths as close as 30 minutes by bus from Granada. Hence, one day in Granada is too short to see all the beauty in and around this city. Yet, if your time is limited, spare at least one or one and a half days for the most spectacular spots in Granada.

How to get to Granada

From Malaga, there are frequent bus connections that take about 2.5 hours. From the bus station, you can catch the local bus 33 to the city center (cathedral). From the train station, it would only be a 1.5 km walk or you can catch any bus along Avda de Constitucion in direction of the cathedral.

In case you travel by car, you can check for free parking spots around *C. Doctor Buenaventura Carreras* near the Neptuno Shopping Center. Then, you take a bus to the city center or start your sightseeing tour by walking for about 25 minutes.

From the airport, you can catch an ALSA bus. The bus station is about a 10-minute walk in front of the airport. The ride into the city takes about 45 minutes and costs 3 EUR. A taxi will only take around 20 minutes and costs 25 to 30 EUR.

How to use the local buses

To get up on a hill you might want to use a public bus. A single ride costs 1.40 EUR. If you are several people or will ride more than 4 trips, you can buy a bus card for 2 EUR. It can be used for more than one person. Then the individual trips only cost about 90 cents.

More information about bus travel in Granada you find on this website: https://www.lovegranada.com/transport/alhambra-buses/

What to do in Granada

The obvious reason to come to Granada is the Alhambra castle. Yet, there are many more beautiful locations to discover but let's start with what you need to know for your Alhambra visit.

Visit the Alhambra and the Generalife

You see the ancient castle towering above the city from the city center or the viewpoints. Inside you find many different sections consisting of palaces, watchtowers, summer residences, and the stunning Generalife gardens. To see everything at a relaxed pace, you will need about 3 hours.

You can get to the Alhambra by walking from Plaza Nueva in 15 minutes. It's a nice walk and although it's uphill, it's doable. The return walk will be quicker as it's all downhill. The same goes for the access via the path marked as *Cuesta del Rey Chico* from Paseo de los Tristes.

If walking uphill isn't your thing, you can catch bus C30 from *Plaza de Isabel la Católica*.

The general entrance to the different buildings costs 18 EUR per adult. The ticket includes the Alhambra, Nasrid Palaces, Generalife, Carlos V Palace, and The Bath of the Mosque. You have to buy the ticket on the following website beforehand: https:comprartickets.alhambra-patronato.es/

When we arrived at the entrance at 3 p.m. with our IDs and pre-purchased tickets, there was already a sign there saying that there were no more tickets available for today. This was on a normal Tuesday. So, buy your ticket early.

You have to select a time slot for the Nasrid Palaces where you will have to enter at exactly this time. The palace is marked on maps.me as *Palacios Nazaries*. For the rest of the places, there is no time limit with your daily ticket except for the opening hours of the Alhambra. The area consists of several entrances, and you also have to scan your ticket again and again, which I found a bit tedious.

The usual opening times are from 8.30 a.m. to 6 p.m. (winter)/ 8 p.m. (summer) but you can also book night tours and see additional evening opening hours on this website: www.alhambra-patronato.es/en/visit/opening-hours-and-prices
After marveling at the buildings for a while, sit down in one of the beautiful courtyards or somewhere in the Generalife and find even more stunning angles to take pictures of this exotic place.

Also take time to visit the small Alhambra Museum in the *Palace of Charles V*, which by the way is located outside the ticket area. That's why you can enter this palace for free without a ticket, in case you missed buying one. There are some beautiful Moorish artifacts in the exhibit. The museum is free, as is the Museum of Fine Arts (free for EU citizens, otherwise 1.50 EUR).

Garden lovers should add one more stop before returning to the center by heading to *Carmen de los Martires Gardens*. The walk takes a little over 10 minutes. They are free to enter and there are many romantic places or pretty fountains and plants. Beware of the opening hours: In winter: Monday to Friday from 10 a.m. to 2 p.m. and 4 p.m. to 6 p.m. and in summer until 8 p.m. Saturdays and Sundays from 10 a.m. to 6 / 8 p.m.

Things to do around Plaza Nueva

Back in town, you are probably hungry. You could visit **Mercado San Augustin**. There are various food stalls with delicious tapas or fresh food to bring home and cook. Otherwise, you can go to **Bib-Rambla Square** where you find many restaurants. On your way, you can walk past the impressive **cathedral of Granada**. It costs 5 EUR to visit including an audio guide. If you want to visit it for free and won't behave like a tourist, you can attend a service. For example, at 10 a.m. on Sunday.

In case you are up for more foreign culture, visit the **Alcaiceria Bazaar** which is right in front of the cathedral. You will feel like on a small Moroccan souk.

If you feel like clothes shopping, head down **Calle Mesones** where you find all the famous national brands.

Stroll down Carrera del Darro and the Paseo de los Tristes

Those are the two prettiest pedestrian walking streets of Granada. You will walk along the Darro River with a lush, romantic flora in the riverbed and cute stone-arch bridges that cross the river. Also along those streets, you can sit down in various inviting **tapas bars**. So, it's definitely a nice neighborhood to be in the early evening.

Also in this area, **the Bañuelo** is situated. It's an ancient Arabic Bathhouse. It consists of three rooms that are used as a museum today, but you still get a good impression of what it used to look like. It's a pretty building and free to enter on Sundays. Otherwise, it's 2.20 EUR to visit and the visit only takes about 5 minutes.

Great places to watch the sunset

The most famous viewpoint in Granada is **Mirador de San Nicolás**. It's right next to the white San Nicolás church of which you can use the tower as a reference point when you are walking toward the mirador from the city center. The walk will take you about 15 minutes and leads through pretty alleys. There are restaurants up there to calm your hungry stomach or thirsty tongues. Enjoy the spectacular view over Granada and the Alhambra. If you don't want to walk there, you can take microbus C31 or C32 from Plaza Isabel Católica.

A less popular sunset viewpoint, perhaps because the walk there takes 10 minutes longer, is **Mirador de San Cristobal**. It's just as beautiful as Mirador de San Nicolás or has even more charm because it's smaller. From Plaza Nueva you can catch bus C34 to get to the mirador.

One more nice area to be strolling through in the golden hour and have something to drink is **Sacromonte**. It's a neighborhood with many white houses that all have different shapes and sizes. Apart from the restaurants, what is even more interesting about those buildings are the underground caves. In many of them, you can watch Flamenco shows in the evening, starting at 20 EUR per person. To reach Sacromonte you can catch bus C31, C32, or C34 from Plaza Nueva. If you walk from the city center, it takes about 20 minutes.

Enjoy Granada after dark

With all those beautiful ancient monuments, Granada also looks beautiful after dark, when most of the buildings are lit up. You could take a guided tour of the Alhambra in the evening at an additional cost, or you can simply enjoy the views in a restaurant in Sacromonte or of the cathedral in the center. As mentioned above, a great evening activity in Granada is watching a Flamenco show. There are also plenty of options in the city center that aren't taking place in a cave. Some start at 15 EUR per person. In case you feel like something different to Spanish food, try a restaurant in the Albaicin area, where you can find delicious tajine (stew in a hot ceramic pot with very flavorful sauces).

Be enchanted by Marbella

Marbella is known as a town where the rich and beautiful like to spend their holidays. I completely understand why they are drawn to this picturesque gem by the sea. Even the sand looks whiter here than in Malaga. The beauty of the alleys reminds me of Cartagena in Colombia. Yet, it really isn't a place that is only reserved for famous stars. Also as a normal tourist, you will have a fabulous time in Marbella and can either treat yourself to luxury in a beautiful boutique hotel or golf resort or find a place suitable to your budget.

How to get to Marbella

From Malaga, you reach Marbella by bus in one hour or by car in 50 minutes. Hence, it can be easily done as a day trip. However, since it's so pretty, I would actually spend some nights here and perhaps take day trips from here to Gibraltar and Ronda instead of from Malaga.

What to do in Marbella

In Marbella you can enjoy strolls along the beach, swimming, or sunbathing.

Discover the instagrammable alleys

No matter where you walk, you will discover a beautiful corner and hence you should get lost in the old town for a while. The most beautiful streets are *Calle Gloria, Calle Carmen, and Calle Misericordia*. In addition, you should have a look at the old castle wall and the pretty *Iglesia de la Encarnación*. The center of town is at *Plaza de los Naranjos* where you also find nice restaurants and cafés.

Sip a glass of cava or wine with some tapas and watch people

Marbella has many great tapas places and with such a beautiful view of the beach or the pretty old town, it's nice to simply sit there and let your gaze wander.

Explore the beaches

There is a boardwalk and cycling path that leads along the coast for 15 km. Go as far as you like and enjoy the nature and different beaches. Apart from swimming and sunbathing at the flat and safe beaches, you can also rent jet skis and SUP boards in some places or go wakeboarding.
The most beautiful beaches are Bounty Beach, Playa de Alicate, and Playa Real de Zaragoza. **Bounty Beach** (the actual name is Playa del Cable, but it's now nicknamed after the

beach bar) is close to the center of Marbella with good facilities and good music. **Playa de Alicate** also offers all the facilities you need for a beach day, including a beach club. The sand is fine, and the beach stretches across a long area. **Playa Real de Zaragoza** is one of the biggest beaches in the area and you will always find a beautiful, empty patch of sand to place your towel on the soft, golden ground. Because of the big space, it seems less crowded and busy.

Have a BBQ at the beach

Even after sunset, the beaches stay alive with people in a good mood. The great thing is since you are on holiday, you don't even have to lift a finger and bring BBQ equipment to the beach. You will see several big BBQ areas where sardines and meat will be grilled for you to perfection. Just follow the smoky smell.

Stroll down Avenida del Mar – Marbella's outdoor sculpture gallery

Along this pedestrian street that is lined with palm trees, you find various sculptures that were made by the artist *Salvador Dali*. A great example of free, public art.

Just a usual indoor museum, nevertheless one that is absolutely worth a visit, is the *Ralli Museum (right next to the Iberostar Hotel)*. It showcases a big collection of famous artists from all over the world like Joan Miró (Spain), Salvador Dalí (Spain), Marc Chagall (Russia), Giorgio de Chirico (Italy), and Lam (Cuba). One more benefit in case you're not entirely convinced yet; the entry is completely free. It's closed on Sunday and Monday but otherwise, open from 10 a.m. to 3 p.m.

Marvel at the yachts in Puerto Banús

This is one of the ports with the most luxurious boats along the Andalusian coast. It's a fantastic place for a sunset drink and feeling beautiful in your prettiest summer clothes.

You can walk the whole way from Marbella to Puerto Banús (7.5 km). It's part of the stunning promenade walk. Or you opt for the L-79 Avanza bus from the bus station that will take you there in 15 minutes for about 2.50 EUR. A taxi will cost approximately 15 EUR.

On weekends in summer, you will frequently encounter outdoor markets in the Puerto Banús area.

If you don't want to go so far but still wish to enjoy a nice location during sunset, have a glass of wine or a cocktail at the *Belvue Rooftop Bar* of the *Amàre Beach Hotel*.

Treat yourself to a delicious meal at El Patio restaurant in the Marbella Club Hotel

This exclusive hotel with its own private section on the beach also has several good restaurants and bars. We indulged one evening at the El Patio restaurant (www.marbellaclub.com/eat-and-drink/el-patio). The tables are in a pretty, green courtyard and those who prefer to dine indoors can also head to the lovely interior rooms. We were greeted with an appetizer (labneh dip with olives and flatbread) and from the start we were kindly taken care of by the attentive waiters. The concept of sharing applies to the appetizers, and it is best to order several appetizers for the entire table. We had oysters, grilled eggplant, and artichokes on a vinaigrette. Everything was so delicious that I would have loved to have tasted my way through the entire appetizer menu. For the main course followed a Wagyu steak with potatoes and grilled octopus for my husband. The cocktails that accompanied our meal were also not ordinary and very tasty.

Another highlight followed at the end, and I had one of the best chocolate cakes of my life. Believe me, I have tried many chocolate cakes. I would return to El Patio restaurant just for this dessert.

Before dinner, we visited the Kids Club at the Marbella Club Hotel with our daughter. From the age of 4, children are looked after with an entertaining program. Younger children may also play there if accompanied by their parents. It's a paradise for kids of all ages with a kitchen, a garden, climbing frames, various playrooms, and all sorts of vehicles or stuffed animals. In addition, the facility is very airy and the children will spend most of the day outside in the shade. So if you would like to put your child in good care for a day while you enjoy the beach or Marbella, or just let your child play as they please, you can register them on the Kids Club website: www.marbellaclub.com/kids-club.

Shop until you drop at La Cañada

This is a big shopping center with an airy design and lots of plants. It's an inviting place to hide out from the heat and enjoy the many shops with well-known brands, restaurants, bars, and cafés.

Visit Ronda

Ronda offers one of those sights that you will see on a picture, and you know you just have to travel there to witness this spectacular place with your own eyes. I am talking about the *Puente Nuevo* that bridges the 120 m deep gap between the new town and the old citadel. It's such a special sight because the pillars of the bridge lead down to the base of the gorge.

How to get to Ronda

The easiest way to visit Ronda is by renting a car and driving from Malaga (1.5h), or Marbella (1h 10 mins). If you want to spend a night in Ronda, you could also continue to Cadiz from Ronda, taking the scenic route (1h 45 mins). Then, you should stop by the ruins of *Acinipo* about 20 km from Ronda and also check out some of the wineries in the area.

If you don't have a car, you can still visit Ronda as part of a day trip by public transport. From the bus station in Marbella, you can take an Avanza bus three times a day for 6.90 EUR (https://booking.avanzabus.com/web/step1.php). The drive takes 1h10 mins. From Malaga, there is one bus in the morning that takes 2h 40 mins and prices start at 13.65 EUR. You could return at 4.30 p.m. Alternatively you can take a train via Antequera which takes about 2 hours.

What to do in Ronda

Of course, you have to admire the bridge and take a few photos. The best view of the bridge is from a steep walkway that starts at the *El Morabito* restaurant (Plaza Maria Auxiliadoria). About halfway between the road and the foot of the bridge, you'll see the bridge along with a waterfall. Really a fabulous sight! However, we saw some people who put their lives in danger by climbing just to take a picture. It would be a great pity if in the future this place is also monitored like El

Caminito del Rey, just because tourists overestimated themselves.

Afterward, you should take a walk in the old town and visit the pretty *Iglesia del Espíritu Santo*. For the best view, go to *Mirador de Ronda*. Then, enjoy the pretty alleys in the old town, the cafés, and the views of the countryside.

If you are looking for a paradise-like place to cool off, drive the 20 minutes to *The Cueva de Gato*. They are clear, turquoise pools in front of a cave with a waterfall.

Visit Gibraltar

Gibraltar is a picturesque town by the sea that is above all famous for a 400 m high rock. From the walks you can do on the rock, you have a great view across the sea (here is where the Mediterranean Sea opens up into the Atlantic Ocean) and can even see the coast of Morocco. It isn't just a town in the South of Spain but actually its own country. It's under British rule and the local currency is the British pound. The city has a British feel to it, and you even find an Irish street with many

Irish pubs. You also have to pass a border checkpoint when visiting Gibraltar. Therefore, you need a valid passport, and, on this website, you can check if you need a visa: http://www.gibraltarborder.gi/visa

Normally, it's no problem to visit Gibraltar for a day or spend some nights there. However, if there are any covid regulations in place, it complicates things since the regulations might not be the same that Spain requires. The current requirements can be looked up on this website: www.gov.uk/foreign-travel-advice/gibraltar/entry-requirements

Now that the administrative things are settled, let's have a look at how to get to Gibraltar and what to do there.

How to get to Gibraltar

By car you need to drive to the border town in Spain; **La Linea**. There, you pass the border and arrive in Gibraltar. The border is open 24h every day.

By bus, you also travel to La Linea. From Malaga, it takes about 2h 45 minutes with Avanza and costs around 14 EUR. If you travel from Marbella, it takes only 1h 15 mins and costs around 7 EUR. From the bus station in La Linea, you can walk to the border as it's just around the corner. In order to get to the city center, you can walk the 3 km or take a local bus. They leave every 7 minutes and cost 2.10 EUR or £1.40.

What to do in Gibraltar

The obvious thing to do in Gibraltar is to hike up to the **Rock Nature Reserve** or take a cable car. You will have a stunning view across the sea. In addition, the nature reserve is the only place in Europe, where you can spot wild monkeys (barbary macaques). This alone is something special. However, newly added suspension bridges and thrill walks from where you can enjoy the view from many different angles, make the package even better.

The walk up to the top takes about 1 hour if you take it slow. In case you don't want to sweat, take the cable car. One-way costs £28.00, including the ticket to the Rock Nature Reserve. A return ride including the nature reserve is £30.00. Just the entry fee for the nature reserve is £13. It includes all the sights on the rock and below the rock like the WWII Tunnels, Apes' Den, the Mediterranean Steps, the nature trails, the Skywalk, the Moorish Castle, the Lime Kiln, the 100 Ton Gun, and Windsor Suspension bridge.
The **WWII Tunnels** are well preserved underground tunnels which are now a fascinating tourist attraction.

Cádiz

We are leaving the Mediterranean Sea and are arriving at the Atlantic Ocean. Cadiz is a picturesque seaside town, with mostly white and sand brown buildings. You can enjoy fresh seafood like fish and oysters and go Spanish sherry tasting while watching beautiful sunsets.

How to get to Cádiz

By car, you can drive directly from Ronda to Cadiz in 1h 45 mins. By bus, it's also possible with *Transportes Comes*. It takes 3.5h and costs about 17 EUR. From Malaga, it takes 5.5 hours via Marbella and prices start at 20 EUR with Avanza. Much closer it is from Seville, from where it only takes 1h 45 minutes with Transportes Comes and prices start at 11 EUR. By train, it takes about the same amount of time but is slightly more expensive. Even from Madrid, you can reach Cadiz directly. The bus ride takes 8h to 9h and prices start at 40 EUR. By train, it's quicker and only takes 4h 20 minutes, starting at 60 EUR.

Note that from Cadiz to Malaga there are only two bus departures per day. Currently, these were at 7 a.m. and 3.30p.m.

What to do in Cádiz

Apart from the beach life and wandering around the pretty old town, there are many cultural and historical sites to be discovered.

Relax or surf at the beaches

The town beach is called *Playa La Caleta*. It's small, pretty, and safe. Also, it's usually quite crowded but still a great place if you just want to dip your toes in the sand or water. If you want to spend more time at the beach, head to *Playa de la Victoria*. That one is more than 2 km long and counts as one of the most beautiful urban beaches in Spain. You will have enough space to yourself but can still enjoy the beach bars or rent a surfboard. The area around Cadiz is getting more and more popular for surfing since the waves can be as good as at Portugal's Algarve coast or up North around San Sebastian. However, it's not very crowded here yet. A very pretty place for a drink on the beach is the glass Beach Club Chiringuito Potito. This is the pure vacation feeling.

For the food lovers

The oldest covered central food market of Spain is situated in Cadiz. Go there in the morning to see mountains of fresh seafood and buy some fresh oysters or fried shrimps to snack on. Apart from that, you find the usual fruit, vegetables, and olives at the *Mercado Central*. It was one of my favorite markets in Spain. The busiest time was around lunchtime from 11 a.m. to 1 p.m. You can also buy fresh seafood at the market stalls and then have it prepared (deep-fried or fried) for about 4 EUR extra in the restaurant on the second floor.

However, there also are many other delicious food stalls where you can choose something. At the entrance there was a sign on which the opening hours of the Mercado Central were noted. According to this, the market should have been open again in the evening. Unfortunately, it was closed then. Fortunately, directly in front of the market is a stand with extremely delicious and very cheap churros (*Churreria la Guapa*). The stand is open in the morning and then again from about 5.15 to 7 p.m. You'll recognize it by the long queue of people waiting in line for the churros.

After having built a foundation in your stomach, you can proceed to one of the sherry tasting bars. Sherry is made of white grapes and called Jerez in Spanish. It's produced in the regions around Cadiz. A good place in the old town to go and taste some local sherry is *Manzanilla*. They serve you the sherry wine right out of the wooden barrels and that gives the bar a cool atmosphere. You should start with the dry ones and continue to the sweet ones, but the staff will gladly make some recommendations. Tasting prices range from 1 to 6 EUR.

For the church lovers

I say it for almost every cathedral in Spain, but once more, the cathedral of Cadiz is absolutely worth seeing. The special feature is a painted red carpet that leads to the entrance. It is also beautiful from the inside. You can visit the cathedral for 4 EUR or pay 6 EUR and also climb on the bell tower, from which you have a good view across the city and the ocean.

For the history lovers

Landmarks that you should visit on a walk around Cadiz are the *Puerta de Tierra* (entrance in the old city wall), the *Museum of Cadiz* (it showcases archeological artifacts and fine arts paintings and some modern paintings, for example, by Miro. It is free for EU citizens and otherwise 1.50 EUR. It is open from Tuesday to Saturday from 9 a.m. to 9 p.m. and on Sunday from 9 a.m. to 3 p.m.). My favorite sight was the *Roman Theater (Teatro Romano)* since you can visit the theater from above as well as the corridor below the theater. The visit to the theater and the small museum is free.

Get some shade in the Parque Genovés

This public park welcomes you with nicely sculptured trees and a small pond with artificial waterfalls. It's a good place if you need some shade or want to relax your eyes after squinting in the glistering waves at the ocean for too long.

Sevilla

Seville is the biggest city in southern Spain and has so much beautiful architecture to offer that your eyes might tear up.

It's a great place to really experience everything Andalusia is famous for, and this in one single city. Watch Flamenco, eat delicious tapas, drink wine, sherry, or taste olive oil. Visit cathedrals, churches, and mesmerizing squares, and join busy Spanish festivities such as the Feria de Abril, the Semana Santa, or a bullfighting event.

How to get to Sevilla

Seville has an international airport and therefore you might arrive directly in Seville from your hometown. The cheapest option to get to the city center is by the special airport bus *EA* which costs 4 EUR one way and 6 EUR return. You can buy the ticket on the bus. It stops at *Plaza de Armas* as well as *Santa Justa train station*. The ride takes 35 minutes.

By taxi, it only takes 15 minutes to reach the city center and costs about 25 EUR.

You can also get to Seville from Cordoba in 1h 20 mins by train starting at 15 EUR. From Madrid, it takes only 2h 40 mins by train, starting at 55 EUR. Flying might be cheaper but the train involves less hassle and is better for the environment. The bus from Madrid takes 6.5 hours, starting at 35 EUR.

From Malaga, you have one bus in the evening that takes 2h 45 mins and costs around 18 EUR with Rede Expressos. Trains leave more frequently and take 2 or 3 hours via Cordoba. Prices start at 22 EUR / 43 EUR.

Riding the local bus or tram: One trip costs 1.40 EUR and you can pay it to the bus driver. You could also buy a 1-day tourist card for 5 EUR or a 3-day card for 10 EUR with unlimited rides. Or you purchase a refundable public transport card for 1.50 EUR from a kiosk and then a trip only costs 69 cents (or 76 cents if you change the bus during the same journey).

What to do in Sevilla

Seville has so many beautiful attractions, that it would be a shame to only spend one day in this city. Since there are many tourists in Seville and all of them visit the same sights, you will encounter long lines in front of the ticket offices. However, it's possible to buy the tickets online for all of the monuments for the same price or even at a reduced rate. So, check out the links in this travel guide before you waste time waiting somewhere for half an hour or more.

Visit the cathedral of Sevilla and Giralda tower

This is the biggest gothic church in the world. Hence, if you don't really like churches, you can skip all the other ones in Andalusia but definitely should have a look at this palace city. The size impresses from the outside and the rich decorations inside are eye-catching. The highlight is to visit the beautiful roof as part of a guided tour. That one costs 21 EUR if you buy it online (https://catedraldesevilla.entradasdemuseos.com). The normal visit including the church tower (Giralda Tower) costs 11 EUR. There used to be free time slots for the visit but at the time of writing, they were suspended, probably due to covid. So, keep your eyes peeled, because also for the free visits, you had to reserve the ticket online.

Your only chance of a free visit is if you enter the cathedral to attend a mass service. You can check the times online: https://www.catedraldesevilla.es/culto/horarios-de-misa/ It's not possible to walk around the church during mass or visit the tower but you can still get an impression of the church.

Enjoy the view from the Metropol Parasol (Setas de Sevilla)

I really liked this futuristic observation deck, though I think the price of admission to the roof is a bit expensive, as there are many other great views in Seville. It reminded me of something you would find in a large Asian metropolis, but because the structure is made of wood instead of shiny steel, I think it fits Seville perfectly. The Setas de Sevilla look like giant umbrellas or mushrooms. Outdoor escalators take you to a free observation deck, where locals also gather to eat their packed lunch or ride skateboards. For 15 EUR you can go to the roof of the mushrooms, with the winding walkways. Your admission is valid for two visits. One during the day and a second in the evening between 9 and 9.30 p.m., when the platform is colorfully illuminated. Buy your ticket here and check out the opening hours:
https://setasdesevilla.com/en/prices-and-times

Marvel at Plaza de España

Wow, this square with the beautiful palace-like building is a must-visit in Sevilla! The great thing is, that you can take it all in from the outside for free and I would say with the picturesque canal and garden it can even be compared to Versailles in Paris and Venice in Italy combined! Along the building you find colorful tile benches that represent all the provinces of Spain. You can take a ride in a horse carriage or sometimes, there are spontaneous tango shows with live music or sports classes taking place in the shade of the archways. Today, the building is mostly used as government offices. Don't miss the chance to take an extended stroll in the picturesque Maria Luisa Park in front of the Plaza de España.

Visit the Real Alcázar

Not only is it a beautiful building with Moorish and Arabic influences but the palace is actually still used by the Spanish royal family today, whenever they are in Sevilla. You will see beautiful arched doors with star windows, and green courtyards with fountains. The entry fee is 13.50 EUR but it's free on Mondays from 6 p.m. to 7 p.m. from April to September, and from 4 p.m. to 5 p.m. from October to March. The Alcázar and the cathedral both lie in the very picturesque Santa Cruz neighborhood. It is filled with colorful buildings and tapas bars. So, be sure to spend some time strolling through the alleys on foot and sitting down in a café or bar.

More architectural sights that you should visit in Sevilla

On a city walk, be sure not to miss the following buildings. Close to the Alcázar you find the *General Archive of the Indies* (Archivo General de Indias). The archive looks pretty from the outside and inside and since it's free to enter, you should take that opportunity. Unfortunately, the important documents from the archives are stored away, like how Columbus calculated the latitude. It is closed on Monday. Another important monument of the city is the *bullfighting arena (La Maestranza)*. You can enter the museum and the arena for 10 EUR if there is no event going on. Close to the arena, you find *El Torre del Oro (golden tower)*. You can walk along the river and especially during sunset, you can take absolutely stunning pictures with this building. You can enter it for free on Monday, otherwise, it costs 3 EUR.

Further, the **Casa de Pilatos** offers beautiful architecture. It attracts fewer tourists than the Alcázar and therefore you have more space to yourself. It costs 10 EUR for the first floor or 12 EUR for both floors with a free audio guide. The visit is free on Monday from 3 p.m. to 7 p.m. Last but not least you need to visit **Plaza del Cabildo**, which is a square with a rounded building. It also looks nice after dark when the building is illuminated.

Marvel at paintings in the Museum of Fine arts

This is the second biggest art museum in Spain after the Prado in Madrid. It's open from 9 a.m. to 3 p.m. every day except Mondays. Admission is free for EU citizens and otherwise it only costs 1.50 EUR. You can see paintings by Velázquez, El Greco, and José de Ribera amongst others.

Wander through the colorful Triana neighborhood and fill your belly at the Mercado de Triana

First, take a picture of the colorful buildings along the river from the center part of town. Then cross the Guadalquivir River and visit the houses from up close. One stop you have to make is at the Triana market, which is a popular local food market. It is open every day from 9 a.m. to 5 p.m. except on Sunday, when it's open from noon to 5 p.m. This is also a great neighborhood to watch an authentic Flamenco show.

Visit the Museo del Baile Flamenco

If you want to see more than just a Flamenco show, you should pay a visit to this museum. It's open every day from 12.30 p.m. to 6.30 p.m. and there is a daily show at 7 p.m. If you only visit the museum, it costs 10 EUR and if you want a combined ticket with the hour-long show, which takes place in a pretty cellar, it is 28 EUR.

Have a fun day at La Isla Magica

This is Sevilla's adventure and aqua park. There are many water rides and one big thrill roller coaster plus many relaxing family rides. If you buy the ticket online, it costs 24 EUR for adults for one day. Check out the special offers online and get discounts for shorter visits: www.islamagica.es/en/prices-and-promotions/. La Isla Magica is in the suburbs of Sevilla, and you can reach it by bus line C1 or C2.

Enjoy local festivities

The two biggest festivals in Seville are the **Semana Santa** and the **Feria de Abril**. The Semana Santa starts on Palm Sunday, leading up to Easter Monday. Different church brotherhoods make processions through the city each day with richly, religiously decorated floats and many people wear traditional clothes. If you are in Spain or especially Seville during Semana Santa, you will need to pre-book your accommodation a long time in advance.

The other big festival is the April fair which takes place two weeks after Easter, so in 2024 from 14. to 20. April and in 2025 from 4. to 10. May. Imagine it like the Spanish version of the Oktoberfest in Munich. Women wear Flamenco dresses, and guys traditional suits and all is decorated with pretty light bulbs. There are many tents in which you can drink or eat tapas. Bullfights, Flamenco shows, and fireworks take place. It's free to visit the colorful booths but some tents you can only visit with an invitation. This festival is definitely a highlight in Andalusia if you can manage to get a room during that week.

Where to stay in Sevilla

The beautiful Hotel Casa 1800 Sevilla (www.hotelcasa1800sevilla .com/) is located in the heart of the city, right next to the cathedral of Sevilla. On the rooftop terrace, you therefore probably have the best view in the city, which you can enjoy from a lounge chair or the saltwater pool which is open all year around. I mean, with this view, the very comfortable bed sheets, and the afternoon tea with tasty pastries, you might not want to leave the hotel at all.

This boutique hotel has 33 royally furnished rooms and suites. My room had a bubble function in the bathtub and some of the suites come with a private jacuzzi on the terrasse, including a view of the cathedral. I received a friendly welcome from the staff, who offered me something to drink right away and were very attentive the whole time. In my room, I was surprised with a bottle of good cava and a plate with incredibly delicious Iberian ham and cheese. Despite being within walking distance of all the major sights of Sevilla and in the middle of busy tapas bars, my hotel room was very quiet, so we had a great sleep. For breakfast, there is a lot of fresh fruit, good meat, and even churros with the real thick chocolate that you would get at a churreria.

With all this service and quality, it's out of the question. Whether it's for a city trip or a longer stay, I will definitely be back at Casa 1800 Sevilla.

Córdoba

Córdoba is rich in Islamic history what is evident in the mosque and Arabic baths. Also, there is a Jewish neighborhood, and of course, you find the usual Spanish influence with Flamenco and tapas. Hence, it's a very culture rich city and, therefore, deserves a spot in this travel guide. In addition, Córdoba simply is beautiful, especially in spring, when most facades are being decorated with flowerpots and you can smell the scent of orange trees in the air.

How to get to Córdoba

From Seville you reach Córdoba in 45 minutes by train, starting at 14 EUR. From Madrid, you reach Córdoba in a little under 2 hours, starting at 42 EUR by train or 5 hours by bus for 30 EUR.

From Malaga, the direct train takes 1 hour and starts at 30 EUR. The quickest bus from Malaga takes 2.5 hours, starting at 17 EUR.

What to do in Córdoba

Córdoba is a city you should mostly explore on foot since there are so many nice alleys, courtyards, and flowers to be discovered. One day is enough to see the main attractions.

Visit the mosque-cathedral (Mezquita de Córdoba)

This monument is said to be the most important Islamic heritage building in the Western world. Over time it was used by Christians and Muslims and today the beautiful architecture can be visited from the inside. The entry fee is 8 EUR and if you want to climb to the top of the minaret, it costs an additional 2 EUR.

In the morning, the visit is free between 8.30 and 9.30 a.m. Arrive early as there usually is a queue. I stayed at the *Hotel Casa Turistica La Torre* just in front of the Mezquita, which was the perfect location for the morning visit. In addition, the Taberna Rafaé around the corner has an extremely tasty Salmorejo and other good Spanish food.

Two more important monuments with nice gardens and fountains are the Alcázar de los Reyes Cristianos and Palacio de Viana. *Alcázar de los Reyes Cristianos* is closed on Mondays and the visit costs 5 EUR. *Palacio de Viana* is also closed on Mondays and costs 10 EUR to enter if you want to see the courtyards and the interior of the small palace.

The most Spanish looking square in Córdoba is *Plaza de la Corredera*. The four-story high buildings with an even pattern of windows surround the square on which you have several cafés and restaurants. Be sure to try a *Salmorejo* while in Córdoba as it is a local specialty. It's like a gazpacho (cold tomato soup) but they add shreds of serrano ham and egg. It is perfectly refreshing on hot days.

Walk around the Jewish neighborhood

This is the nicest area in Córdoba because here the residents put a lot of effort into decorating their houses with flowerpots. For example, the *Calleja de las Flores* is pretty or *Calleja del Indiano*.

In the second and third week of May, people even open their private courtyards so that visitors can have a look at the pretty gardens in hidden alleys. This is part of the *Patios de Córdoba* festival and a great time to visit Córdoba. Another good time if you would like to celebrate is to come during

Córdoba's smaller version of the Feria de Abril in Seville. The Feria de Córdoba takes place in the last week of May. The fairgrounds also get richly decorated with light bulbs and the people dress up in Flamenco clothes to walk through the booths that offer goods. Visiting the fairgrounds is free.

Marvel at the Roman Bridge

This bridge has a nice architectural structure and also looks good in the evening, when it is illuminated. On the other side of the river, you see the *Calahorra Tower* which was built as a defense tower.

Madrid

Madrid is the capital of Spain. It has the most inhabitants and there is a huge airport from which you can find cheap flights to many cities in Europe, Spain itself, or South America.

The historic center is possible to visit on foot. Since there are so many beautiful buildings and parks to see, walking is the best method to see Madrid anyway. However, with all the different popular neighborhoods and parks, you will need to wear comfortable shoes and you might still be glad to take a shortcut with a bus or metro once in a while. In the historic center, the Spanish holiday mood is palpable as soon as the cafés and tapas bars open their terraces and people start snacking on olives or jamon while sipping on a glass of local wine or beer. The positive vibe is contagious, and you will definitely have a good time in Madrid.

How to get from the airport to the city center

First, let me tell you that I hate Madrid airport. It's so big that no matter whether I am there for a stopover or to actually get off at Madrid, I always have to walk miles and miles between terminals and gates. I am not kidding. This is annoying, especially if you arrive from further away and are tired from traveling. It's not like I haven't been to any other big airports in the world, but somehow, they manage to organize the passenger transits in a better way. So, if you tend to sugar-lows when not sleeping enough, bring an extra power bar on your trip to Madrid for the long walks in the airport.

The quickest way to get to the city center is by **metro**. The most popular stop in the center is *Sol* (Puerta del Sol). To get there, you take metro LINE 8 from terminal 4 to *Nuevos Ministerios* where you change on a metro that goes to Sol. At the airport, there are free trains or shuttle buses between the terminals in case you arrive at a different terminal. There is an airport surcharge of 3 EUR and a single ride metro ticket costs between 1.50 and 2 EUR, depending on how far you ride. So, the total trip will cost you about 4.50 EUR. The ride to the tourist center takes about 25 minutes. You can buy the ticket at the machine at the metro station, where you also have the choice of buying a multi-day public transport ticket. However, since Madrid is great to discover on foot, you probably won't ride the metro or bus enough in order that you get your money's worth.

Be careful not to confuse the metro with the **train** that also leaves from terminal 4 and connects you with *Atocha Station*. The train is slightly cheaper than the metro.

Another quick option is the 203 express bus which will bring you to *Atocha* or *Cibeles* for 5 EUR, but you have fewer options to get off than with the metro.

In case you are staying in a suburb of the city center, a normal public bus might be cheaper and quicker to get to the airport or vice versa. Then, you won't have to pay any airport surcharge and the ticket only costs about 1.50 EUR. Check your connections on Google maps before you get to Madrid because the Wi-Fi at Madrid airport is not reliable.

In case you want to hop on a taxi, the ride will take up to 40 minutes due to traffic jams and it will cost you about 35 EUR.

What to do in Madrid

Madrid offers amazing art museums, beautiful parks, and great tapas bars. Following you find the must-dos for this picturesque city.

Discover the most stunning monuments on a DIY city walk

In Madrid, I walked over 20k steps per day since there simply was so much to see. Some buildings, you really shouldn't miss, and you could visit them in the following order.

Let's start at **Almudena Cathedral** which is as impressive from the outside as it is from the inside. A beautiful picture you can take from the square that the cathedral shares with the **Royal Palace of Madrid** on the other side. From the square terrace, you have a great view across the suburbs of Madrid. Then, we head into the historic city center. You will discover many pretty alleys but two places that you must include on your walk are the glass building of **Mercado de San Miguel** and **Plaza Mayor**. This is a cobblestone square, surrounded with cafés and restaurants in a building with a stunning façade. After getting a bit lost in the many streets filled with tapas bars, you head to **Puerta del Sol** to look at the famous clock tower and can immerse yourself in Madrid's best clothes shops.

From there, you continue to the picturesque city hall, **Palacio de Cibeles**. You can enter the building for 3 EUR to access the viewing platform (Mirador Madrid) from which you have a pretty view over Madrid. Or, have a meal at one of the restaurants on the 6th floor from where you also have a good view.

Now, you are at **Parque Retiro**. The park is huge and, except if you are planning a long jogging route, you won't see the whole park in one day. However, now, you could walk through the park to get to the other end and reach the final spot on this walk, **Atocha train station**. Inside the train station, you find a rainforest jungle garden which makes the station quite special. In case you don't feel like walking there all the way, you can always catch a bus or a metro (to Estacion del Arte).

One more interesting building which you should visit by metro are the KIO towers. They show the modern side of Madrid by being the first leaning skyscrapers in the world.

Have a picknick at Retiro Park

On a sunny day, it's always a good idea to head to Retiro Park, the green lungs of Madrid. Bring a picknick or use one of the many sports facilities. Perhaps you and your partner feel like a romantic boat ride on the lake or visiting the free crystal palace (a beautiful glasshouse)? The park has so many different interesting sections, that it's worth coming back multiple times and not rushing it.

Visit one or several art museums

Like so many other cities in Spain, Madrid is home to several great art museums with world-famous paintings. The best is that most museums offer free visiting hours. The top three museums are The Prado, Reina Sofia Museum, and Thyssen-Bornemisza museum. If you have a teacher ID, you can visit all of them for free. The Reina Sofia Museum and Prado Museum (www.museodelprado.es/en) are free for everyone in the last two hours of the day. For the Reina Sofia Museum (www.museoreinasofia.es/en), you just go there at that time and get a free ticket after waiting in the (probably long) line. It's also possible to get the ticket online. For the Prado, you have to sign up at the counter for a ticket at 10 a.m. of the day you want to visit it in the evening.

In The Prado, you find Las Meniñas by Diego Velazquez, as well as many other Velazquez', Goyas, Bosch', plus a Mona Lisa painting by one of Leonardo DaVinci's students. (Opening hours: Monday to Saturday from 10 a.m. to 8 p.m. Sundays and holidays from 10 a.m. to 7 p.m.)

In The Reina Sofia Museum, you can look at the famous Guernica painting, at many more Picassos, and Dalis. (Opening hours: 10:00 a.m. - 9:00 p.m., closed on Tuesdays, Sunday: 12.30 – 2.30 p.m. (no free time slot).
The Thyssen-Bornemisza Museum (www.museothyssen.org/en) is easier to navigate than the other two museums. You find art from early painters to the present and lots of famous names. I found it more varied than the other two museums. There are no free time slots for this museum. (General entry: 13 EUR, reduced: 9 EUR, Opening hours: 10 a.m. – 7 p.m. except Mondays: 12 p.m. – 4 p.m.)

Enjoy Spanish tapas

You shouldn't spend a day in Spain without having at least one delicacy of a Spanish food variation. In *Calle De Cava Baja* and the surrounding *Latin Quarter,* you find many bars with nice murals on the facades. When the terraces and chairs are filled with people it's a lively spot where you will enjoy spending your evenings. Otherwise, you find good tapas at the touristy *Mercado de San Miguel* or head by metro to the less touristy and more authentic *Mercado de Vallehermoso.* Check the opening times online: www.mercadovallehermoso.es.

Watch a Flamenco show

In case you don't have time to watch Flamenco in Andalusia, where this dance originated, you will find plenty of opportunities in Madrid. Just look out for flyers or ask the staff in your accommodation. Sometimes, you even see street artists presenting a spontaneous Flamenco show, so keep your eyes open.

Where to spend the night in Madrid

The luxurious heaven in the city center: Gran Hotel Inglés

Gran Hotel Inglés (www.granhotelingles.com/) impresses guests with a beautiful, luxurious, and high-quality interior design. The big and comfortable chairs are only one of the many features that make you feel right at home. I received a nice welcome with flavored water and a glass of cava. The staff is very knowledgeable and can answer any questions you might have about Madrid.

My executive room had a big, free-standing bathtub. There was lots of space and the bed had comfortable pillows and very soft sheets. The welcome snacks made my mouth water because they consisted of fresh figs and delicious chocolate mousse bites that were covered with even better chocolate. Then, I dove into exploring the city, as GHI is located right in the center, and you can walk everywhere. Every time I got back to my room, the trash cans were emptied, and it amazed me how attentive the staff was. You really can expect a high quality of service at Gran Hotel Inglés. For the modern gym, you can request a personal trainer and in the spa area, there is a room with a jacuzzi that is let into the ground. You can reserve the jacuzzi for 30 minutes for free and enjoy it by yourselves.

Breakfast was varied and came with Iberian ham and delicious salami. I could continue like this for a while, but in short; I can't stop raving about this beautiful hotel.

Special tip for taco lovers: Right around the corner of the hotel you find *El Chaparrito* Mexican restaurant. It's a very authentic restaurant that has even received an award from the Mexican government. You can have tacos starting at 1 EUR and all the food is very delicious. I went back several times.

If you come by car or need to work: Artiem Hotel

Artiem Hotel (www.artiemhotels.com/artiem-madrid/) will awaken your body and soul after a long traveling day with a fresh and modern design. I even had an Alexa in my room who listened to my orders. Otherwise, the room was spacious and quiet, and you will get a good sleep. The friendly reception staff gave me a great introduction to the hotel and so I learned that a big snack counter can be accessed for free all day. You can enjoy things like olives, healthy salads, yogurt, coffee, tea, and even different fruit juices, beer, and wine. So, if you are busy working with the good WIFI in the nice common area or on their terrace, you don't even have to leave for lunch or dinner. The gym can be accessed 24 hours and has top equipment. Or, if you don't want to train in public, you receive a bag with a yoga mat and other utensils to take to your room.

Artiem Hotel is especially practical if you travel by car since they have free parking spots in a garage, which is rare to find in a Spanish city. By public bus #200 you get to the airport in 20 minutes for 1.50 EUR.

Picture: Plaza Mayor

International connections to Morocco

Without covid restrictions, it's very easy to travel to Morocco from Andalusia, even just for a day trip. You only need a valid passport. The quickest ferry route is from Tarifa (Spain) to Tangier (Morocco) from where you can travel by bus or train to other parts of Morocco. The ferries leave every hour by either *FRS* or *Intershipping* and the crossing takes 35 minutes. Ferry tickets can be bought or compared on this website: https://www.directferries.de/frs.htm

Some useful words in Spanish

English	Spanish
Hello	Hola
How are you?	¿Cómo estás?
I'm well and you?	Bien, gracias y tú?
Where are you from?	¿De donde eres?
I'm from...	Soy de... (Estados Unidos, Inglaterra)
Yes	Si
No	No
Where is the toilet/ATM?	¿Dónde está el baño/cajero?
Thank you.	Gracias
How much is...?	¿Cuánto cuesta...?
Sorry	Lo siento
Please	Por favor
I need to change money.	Necesito cambiar dinero.
I would like...	Me gustaría... / Quiero...
The bill, please.	La cuenta, por favor.
Water	Agua
Chicken	Pollo
Without meat	Sin carne
Enjoy your meal.	Buen provecho.
What time does... arrive?	¿Cuándo llegará...?
Bus	El autobús
Plane	El avión
Boat	El barco
Waterfall	La cascada
Right	Derecha
Left	Izquierda

About the author of this guidebook

Seraina/ SwissMiss onTour loves to travel since she can remember.

It started with beach vacations with her family on Mallorca when she was a child but soon, she sought her own routes. She was lucky to be able to spend an amazing High School year in New York at 15 years old. That's when she started to write her first travel blog which evolved into *SwissMissOnTour*. Later, she explored Europe with Interrail but was also attracted by the exotic countries further away. Countless trips to Southeast Asia made her fall in love with the delicious Asian flavors, beautiful temples, and nature highlights. South America was always at the back of her mind but for that, she wanted to have more time in order not to have to fly back and forth to Switzerland in every vacation. So, when the timing was right, she quit her job and has been fully enjoying the countries of South America. Unfortunately, the coronavirus pandemic has forced her to return to Switzerland earlier than planned. Here, once more, she takes every chance she gets to explore places near and far. Another exciting adventure started in 2022 when her first child was born. Since she also traveled quite a bit during her pregnancy or now with the toddler, feel free to contact her on Instagram if you have any questions or concerns about traveling during pregnancy or with children.

Do you need more info?

In case you need more info, I am happy to help. Contact or follow me through these channels. Especially on Instagram, you can enjoy daily travel tips, inspiration, and travel quotes.

(b) www.swissmissontour.com
(i) @swissmissontour
(f) SwissMissOnTour
(w) www.slgigerbooks.wordpress.com

*By the way, since the photos in this travel guide are black and white, you can send me an e-mail with a picture of the book, and I will send you the e-book version of I love Andalusia for free. In the e-book, the pictures are in color. *

Did you like this travel guide?

In case you liked this travel guide, I'd greatly appreciate a positive review on Amazon, and it would be a good support if you told your friends about it ☺

Scan the QR-code and leave your review.

More books by S. L. Giger

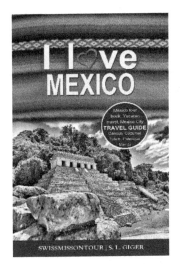

Made in the USA
Middletown, DE
03 October 2023

40090537R00060